John James Audubon

by Judy Nayer

Table of Contents

Who Was John James Audubon?

John James Audubon loved nature. He studied and painted birds in a way that had never been done.

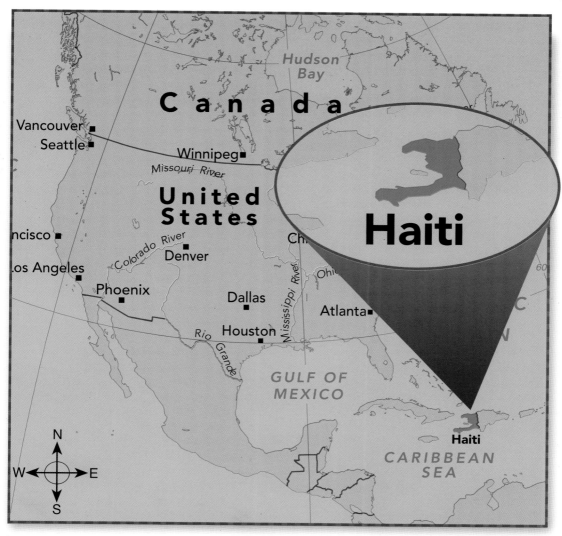

John James Audubon was born on April 26, 1785, on Haiti, an island in the Caribbean Sea. He later moved to France and then to America.

John set out to paint pictures
of as many birds as he could.
John wanted to paint them
as they looked in real life.
He painted pictures of birds eating.

Here is a photo of a grackle. How does it compare
to John's painting of grackles on page 5?

5

He painted pictures of birds
in their nests.

He painted pictures of birds looking for food.

John lived in many places during his life. He painted pictures of the birds that lived near him.

These are some of the birds that John painted at his farm.

Here is one of John's homes.
It was in New York.

John wanted everyone to see birds
the way he did. He put his paintings
in a book. It showed the birds
as big as they were in real life!

Here is a photo of a wild turkey. How does it
compare to John's painting of a wild turkey
on page 11? It is from John's book,
The Birds of America.

How Did John Learn About Birds?

John wanted to see if birds come back
after they grow up and leave
their nests. He looked at baby birds.

He put string around some of
the baby birds' legs. The next spring
he saw some birds with string on
their legs. He learned that some birds
come back to the same place every year.

Scientists use tags to track birds.
It is called banding.

How Did John Help Save Birds?

Soon John saw that people were hunting too many birds and other animals.
He wanted to save the birds and animals.

These birds are passenger pigeons. There were many of them when John was alive. Now there are none.

Some people started a group
to save birds. They named it after John.

The Audubon Society began in 1905.

This group still works hard today
to save birds and other animals.